The Story of the Dee in Wales

FROM BALA TO LLANGOLLEN

Michael Senior

Text © 1990 Michael Senior

ISBN: 0-86381-155-8

Cover: Llangollen Bridge (Photo: Celtic Picture Agency)

Gwasg Carreg Gwalch

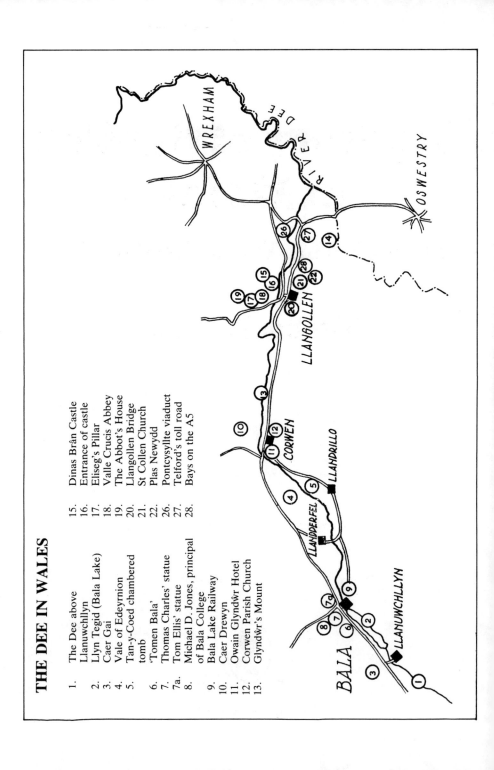

THE DEE IN WALES

1. The Dee above Llanuwchllyn
2. Llyn Tegid (Bala Lake)
3. Caer Gai
4. Vale of Edeyrnion
5. Tan-y-Coed chambered tomb
6. 'Tomen Bala'
7. Thomas Charles' statue
7a. Tom Ellis' statue
8. Michael D. Jones, principal of Bala College
9. Bala Lake Railway
10. Owain Glyndŵr Hotel
11. Caer Drewyn
12. Corwen Parish Church
13. Glyndŵr's Mount
15. Dinas Brân Castle
16. Entrance of castle
17. Eliseg's Pillar
18. Valle Crucis Abbey
19. The Abbot's House
20. Llangollen Bridge
21. St Collen Church
22. Plas Newydd
26. Pontcysyllte viaduct
27. Telford's toll road
28. Bays on the A5

I ORIGINS

I N Welsh the Dee is called the Dyfrdwy, and that is the name it bears in its reaches above Bala lake. The Welsh name is often translated 'the water of the Dee', though this explains little, since both the 'dwy' in this phrase and the name Dee itself derive from an obscure origin. Pennant, in the 18th century, speculated that it came from 'Duw', 'divine', and referred to the river's supposedly sacred nature. He cites the Romano-Celtic river goddess Divona as a continental equivalent.

The Dyfrdwy is one of the three mountain streams feeding the head of the lake, the other two being the Lliw to the west and the Twrch to the east, each draining a massive mountain block, with the Dyfrdwy if anything more modest in the middle. They meet at Llanuwchllyn, 'the parish above the lake', and join there the road up from Dolgellau which follows the line of a Roman highway. A focal quality is enforced by the terrain, and the lake itself is part of the effect.

The Dee in its infancy above Llanuwchllyn is a moderate stream (1), not suggestive of any later sacredness. It ripples through an intimate valley beside the line of the long-closed railway. Pennant says there was a legend that it passes through the lake without its water getting mixed "as the Rhone is fabled to serve the lake of Geneva", but dismisses this attractive fable on the rather pedantic ground that it does not strictly become the 'Dee' until it leaves the lake's foot. In fact at that point and for its total journey it remains also the Dyfrdwy. The Dee may not be strictly capable of passing through the lake unmixed, but yet perhaps the Dyfrdwy could.

Legends abound here, occurring in an atmosphere which is in any case rather otherwordly, affected as it is by elements such as those sudden mists which the lake produces sometimes from its surface, and the general dominance of natural forces, wind and water, hillside and cloud (2). Perhaps these old traditions find a remote descendant in the fervent outbreaks of religious commitment which, as we shall see, are part of the character of Bala, this area's sole (and remote) contact with the familiar reality of urban life. A notable modern descendant or survivor from more mysterious times is the lake's monster, which has been sighted several times in recent years and at present remains unexplained. The surface of that great sheet of water has always, it seems, suggested mysteries.

Though Bala town now is a fairly humble place there was a great city once (the legend says) beneath what is now the lake. The excesses of a wicked king brought about its downfall, and this submergence gives us the fine sheet of water we enjoy today. This is a common and universal folk-tale, the drowned luxurious land, perhaps reflecting partly real memories (since the flooded area has spread in early and pre-historic times over a once-dry

(1) The river Dee above Bala Lake, here known by its Welsh name, Dyfrdwy, is a lively upland stream.

(2) Bala Lake lies in an evocative upland setting.

I ORIGINS

alluvial valley) and partly possibly offering a symbol for our sense of a lost past when life was better than it now is.

This is the stuff of folk-tale, but there are more basic associations in myth in this area. It is interesting that at two points of this journey along the Dee we come across early forms of that magic vessel which came from such diverse origins to become the Holy Grail, the mystical life-giving symbol sought by knights in medieval stories. One of its sites of origin in fact is an island on Bala lake, or Llyn Tegid, to give it its proper name, the 'beautiful lake'.

There lived on this island in mythical times a man called Tegid Foel and his wife Ceridwen, who had two children, Creirwy, the most beautiful girl in the world, and Afagddu, the ugliest boy. In order to compensate the latter for his ugliness Ceridwen decided to make him all-knowing. To do so she set about boiling a cauldron of knowledge and inspiration, the recipe for which she had in an ancient book. Casting into it the appropriate herbs at the right state of the stars, she set in motion one of the most appealing Welsh tales. Doing so she forms for us the pivotal point at which the Celtic sacred vessel which archeology indicates was a widespread and important religious form emerges from its silent past to generate its multiple offspring, life-giving or inspiring vessels still with us today in the form of the Christian chalice and the witch's cauldron.

The cauldron with which Ceridwen has accidentally inspired so many people ironically failed in its purpose of compensating her ugly son. One of the specifications was that it had to boil continuously for a year and a day, when it would yield the reduced potion of three drops of distilled inspiration. Ceridwen therefore put a boy, little Gwion, to stir it. Towards the end of the year, however, the three drops flew out of the cauldron and landed on Gwion's finger. Because they were hot he put his finger in his mouth, and instantly knew everything. Among the things he knew was that Ceridwen would try to destroy him.

There then began a succession of shape-changes which could be taken to refer to the Celtic belief in metampsychosis, the return of the soul in a different body after death. He changes into a hare, she, as a greyhound, pursues him; he sees a river and becomes a fish, but she is after him still as an otter; in the end he hides as a grain of wheat in a barn, but destiny is not so easily avoided. Ceridwen comes scratching among the wheat as a black hen, and swallows him.

Nine months later Gwion is again reborn, and after further fateful events takes up a new life as the inspired prophet Taliesin. The story says, in effect, that the wisdom of the poet Taliesin came from a former life in which he drank of the cauldron of inspiration possessed by the witch-goddess Ceridwen.

This story does not occur in the earliest manuscript sources, but in a

An aerial view of Caer Gai shows the square outline of the Roman fort.

(3) The base of the rampant of the Roman fort of Caer Gai, above Bala, now forms part of a modern enclosure.

I ORIGINS

mid-16th century document, parts of which may have been tampered with later. Lady Charlotte Guest included it in her translation of the Mabinogion, and it is occasionally appended to modern translations, but in spite of its recognisable features of early oral folk tradition it is not usually regarded as forming part of that body of authentic tradition.

That Bala is quiet and remote now is perhaps misleading, since it seems to have started its history as a focal point. The network of Roman roads in North Wales, governed as it was by the terrain, set the structure for later development and communications. The main approach to North Wales lay along the north coast, from the legionary headquarters at Chester to the forts of Canovium on the river Conwy and Segontium on the coast at Caernarfon. From both these centres roads ran southwards, meeting at Tomen-y-Mur near Trawsfynydd and proceeding southwards together from there to reach, eventually, the South-Wales Roman city Maridunum, now Carmarthen. Linking to this was a more southerly spur from Chester via the fort at the head of Llyn Tegid and thence down the valley to join the main road at Dolgellau.

Caer Gai, as the fort is called, lies on a hillside overlooking the valley of the Dyfrdwy and the present road, unusually elevated for a Roman fort (3). In early tradition the name is associated with a figure of British myth, none other than King Arthur's foster-brother Cai, later known as Sir Kay. The Elizabethan poet Spenser, evidently having heard of this tradition, places King Arthur's fosterage in this upper valley of the Dee in his epic 'The Fairy Queen'. From equally early times, however, it was also recognised that Caer Gai was Roman, and Pennant notes that "multitudes of coins have been found in different parts of the neighbourhood". His predecessor Camden, in the 16th century, ascribed the name to a Roman leader Caius, and this may well reflect an accurate record.

Roman it undoubtedly is, whether or not before that (as its hilltop position suggests) a British fort. The wall which is visible from the road is probably part of the Roman fort but improved to its present form to make a retaining wall lining the Roman rampart. This forms a flat terraced area inside the fort, probably a landscaping feature connected with the Tudor manor house which stands at the centre of the fort. This latter was a seat of the Vaughan family, as indeed were several of the larger houses of this area.

There are signs that the Roman road towards Chester set off from the north-east side of the fort, near where the entrance to the farmyard now is. An inscribed stone found in the field on this side indicates that the fort was garrisoned in the early second century A.D. by the First Cohort of Nervii, and other artefacts, burial urns and coins found in a nearby field, indicate occupation at the end of the first century; but we do not know any more about the history of Caer Gai than these slight clues tell us, or than we can guess from its commanding position at the end of the valley with an outlook over a wide stretch of the river.

(4) An old coaching road accompanies the Dee through the wooded Vale of Edeyrnion.

(5) The ruined cromlech of Tan y Coed, between Llandrillo and Corwen, still possesses its impressive capstone.

8

I ORIGINS

Beyond the other end of the lake, above the probable line of the Roman road and the present main road lay a substantial Iron Age fort, Caer Euni, lying at the end of a long steep-sided ridge above the straight and enclosed valley which runs parallel to that of the Dee. The references in place-names in this area to 'Sarn' and 'Sarnau' (usually translated as 'causeway' but often used in connection with Roman roads and ancient trackways) may indicate that Caer Euni overlooked an important route. The location of the fort is also clearly based on its exceptional outlook over a large area and the easily defended position provided by the sheer fall to the valley, and it must have been of some importance in its day since it merited a large extension, a second phase of building.

The Dee itself meanwhile meanders in another broad and gentle valley, the Vale of Edeyrnion, flanked by an old coach road bordered by immense and ancient hedgerow trees, an abundance of natural vegetation all around clearly thriving in the mild and sheltered climate (4). The valley is punctuated by the compact small towns of Llandrillo and Llandderfel, and here too signs of pre-history remain, such as a small hillfort overlooking the junction of the Dee and the Ceidiog valleys, near Llandrillo, and stone circles and cairns in the rising land to the east and at various points on the edges of the Berwyns above the east and south banks of the Dee. The land above the valley near Llandderfel is similarly dotted with early enclosures.

Perhaps the easiest of these artefacts to see is the substantial chambered tomb which lies at the side of the road from Llandrillo to Corwen, a mile and a half from the former, on the left in that direction. Known as Tan-y-Coed, it is in a state of some disorder but its impressive capstone lies on top of it with an air of permanent immovability (5).

It is remarkable to think that these quiet rural places, from Llanuwchllyn to Llandrillo, had seen, from neolithic Tan-y-Coed to Roman Caer Gai, some three thousand years of activity before our history even started.

*An aerial view of Llyn Tegid showing the town of Bala
situated where the river Dee leaves the lake.*

*(6) 'Tomen Bala', probably the mound of a medieval motte-and-bailey castle, is now obscured
by shrubs and surrounded by buildings.*

II BALA

ALA's oldest structure, 'Tomen Bala', has in the past excited curiosity, but today unfortunately invites rather the reverse (6). Hidden by houses and covered in bushes and trees, it is not quite the prominence which it no doubt once was. In Pennant's day its slopes were covered with townspeople knitting, since that was the main industry of the town, and from its top there was a fine view of the lake and the surrounding hills. When George Borrow came, some hundred years later, it was still impressive, described by him as one of "that brotherhood of artificial mounds of unknown antiquity, found scattered, here and there, throughout Europe and the greater part of Asia". While Pennant says it was probably Roman, and the site of a small fort, Borrow inclines to think that before its use as a stronghold, or alternatively a temple, it was a burial mound.

In fact it is probably nothing more exciting than a medieval motte, a form very common in some areas of Wales and the Midlands, represented in these parts by the mound up at the Roman camp of Tomen-y-Mur and another, which we shall shortly see, known as Glyndŵr's Mount, also alongside the river Dee near Carrog (13). These mottes formed the keep section of motte and bailey castles put up, often quite quickly and temporarily, by Norman Marcher lords, a style of military defence connected with the feudal system and the Norman invasion and very common during the twelfth century.

Of course there remains the possibility that whoever constructed the mound at Bala, whether or not a medieval motte, may have made use of an artificial mound of more ancient date. It is known that the vast burial mounds of Ireland were used at later times as defensive positions, and no doubt the feudal lords in building their castles used whatever existing natural or artificial assistance lay to hand.

Who may have fortified medieval Bala is not known, nor is much known about its history in subsequent centuries. It features in the charters of the Welsh princes — Llewelyn the Great is said to have founded a castle there in 1202 — and in connection with the castle at Harlech in the 14th century, so it was almost certainly fortified by alternate sides in the Plantagenet wars of invasion.

By the time Pennant wrote about his journey, in the 18th century, Bala was a thriving producer of woollen goods and a busy market centre for them. Everyone in the town, in his description, was engaged in knitting stockings. The wool, he tells us, came from the Conwy valley market. He noted the regular appearance of Bala's town plan, which made him wonder if it had Roman origins. The name, he says, comes from the word for a river flowing out of a lake.

By George Borrow's time, the mid-19th century, not much had changed.

11

(7) Thomas Charles' statue in Bala's Tegid Street.

(7a) The statue of Tom Ellis, the influential 19th century Liberal M.P., dominates Bala's main street.

12

II BALA

It was a sizeable town then — he estimates three to four thousand as its population — but with the same simple street plan as today. Borrow stayed at the White Lion, where he was impressed by the breakfast. He notes the fervent interest in religion which is one of Bala's chief distinctions, recording the spirited resistance which was made in Bala at that time by the Anglican church against the general upsurge of Methodism.

Bala's flowering came (and went) with the Methodist Revival. The town's connection with this seems to start with an episode in 1800, when a girl called Mary Jones walked thirty miles across the hills barefoot to acquire a bible. The great Thomas Charles of Bala, to whom she came, was obliged to give her his own, and so struck was he by this inequity of demand and supply that he was inspired to found the British and Foreign Bible Society. More influentially even than this, Charles founded the Sunday School movement, to which Welsh rural education owes so much, and also the Welsh Calvinistic Methodist body. It was perhaps his act of personally ordaining the latter's first eight ministers which forms the moment of that powerful movement's birth, in Bala, in 1811. A statue of Charles now stands in Tegid Street (7).

Subsequently Bala became prominent as the centre for the training of Calvinist Methodist ministers. The former college, now the offices of the Welsh Presbyterian Youth Chaplain, is one of Bala's several religious buildings.

Other notable figures in Welsh cultural and social history abound in Bala. Tom Ellis, Member of Parliament for Meirionnydd in the second half of the 19th century, was the inspiration for the radical wing of the Liberal Party, again a movement very much attuned to Welsh attitudes. His statue occupies a more prominent spot than Charles', in the town's main street (7a). The survival of the Welsh language through a time of severe suppresion owes much to a Bala father and son, Sir Owen M. Edwards, founder of *Cymru*, and Sir Ifan ab Owen Edwards who continued his good work on behalf of Welsh language and culture in the early part of this century.

Another remarkable piece of Welsh history originates from Bala. In 1865 the Reverend Michael D. Jones (8), principal of Bala's College of Congregationalists, fitted out a sailing ship, the *Mimosa*, which took 153 men, women and children to Patagonia in South America, in order that they might be able to practise unpersecuted their non-conformist religion, and their language. The result is that there is still in Patagonia a Welsh-speaking colony, one of history's more improbable sagas of heroism and determination and one of its more curious survivals.

Remarkably another now world-famous tradition, the sheep-dog trial, also arose in Bala, the first being held outside the town in 1873.

From all this it will be seen that Bala is quintessentially Welsh. Now no longer linked to the world by railway, and never on any major road route, it

(8) Michael D. Jones of Bala, 1822-1898.

(9) The railway along the lake shore at Bala is now a narrow-gauge tourist attraction.

14

II BALA

has a feeling of remoteness and independence accentuated by one's probable approach over moorland or by winding lane through rolling fields. It is a compact town surrounded by miles of empty upland country.

From this very sound background Bala is now emerging into a new era, that of the booming leisure industry. Possessing as it does the largest inland area of natural water in Wales, it has the assets required to make a visitor's journey worthwhile. Traditionally its vast surrounding moorland made it the centre of the autumn sport of grouse shooting. Now its 1,084 acres of water are helping it to thrive as a site of summertime recreation as well.

Llyn Tegid now offers fishing, sailing, skin-diving and bird-watching, the large variety of wild life retained by an enlightened ban on power boats of all kinds. Among other water birds there are said to be six species of duck, and the herons and cormorants are no doubt gratified by the fourteen species of fish which swim in the lake's brown waters. One, which has survived from the ice age by living at a depth too great for rod or beak, is unique to Llyn Tegid, and unique also in only having a name in Welsh, the Gwyniad.

Even Bala's defunct railway (axed by Beeching in the 1960's) has been reincarnated as a narrow-gauge line, on the original route, which has run along the south shore of the lake since 1972 (9).

Mountain scenery, wool, non-conformism, Sunday schools, sheep-dog trials, the defence of the ancient language, narrow-gauge railways and recreation. It is as if Bala has been chosen to be the representative of all that is most distinctive about North Wales.

(10) Caer Drewyn near Corwen, used over thousands of years as a defensive position.

OWAIN GLYNDWR HOTEL
FORMERLY THE "NEW INN"
◆ CORWEN ◆
THE FIRST EISTEDDFOD TO WHICH THE
PUBLIC WERE ADMITTED WAS HELD IN
THIS HOTEL ON 12ᵀᴴ MAY 1789.

(11) The Owain Glyndŵr Hotel in Corwen was the site of the first National Eisteddfod.
(11a) Commemorative plaque at the Owain Glyndŵr Hotel.

III OWAIN GLYNDŴR

HE Vale of Edeyrnion bears the river Dee down to Corwen, where they both meet the A5. The Dee and its valley in fact do a sudden right-hand bend below the town, while the road curves more gently through it. Here on the northern side of the valley the river passes below a round, commanding hill, the top of which bears an unusually fine example of an Iron-Age hillfort. Caer Drewyn, the walls of which run for half a mile around the hill, forms an enclosure suitable for a sizable tribe. It bears, moreover, powerful associations in Welsh history, since it was there, a thousand years or so after its first use, that the troops of the great Welsh leader Owain Gwynedd are traditionally said to have confronted the army of Henry II encamped across the valley on the Berwyn hills, after (or in some accounts before) the crucial battle of Crogen. Such defensive positions were also used by Glyndŵr in his guerilla warfare, and it is highly likely that this was one (10).

Running through Corwen one will not find a great deal to note, except perhaps the Owain Glyndŵr Hotel (11). Corwen's parish church in fact lies immediately behind that establishment, in a pleasantly secluded setting (12). Attractive from the outside, due partly to its mellow brownish stone, its interior is disappointing, being conventionally restored. A monolith set into the wall of the main porch probably indicates a pre-Christian religious site. A legend (which is in fact an international tale) tells how the builders attempted to raise the church elsewhere, but found their structure demolished each night and the materials moved to the site of the stone. The church's best-known feature is an early cross carved into the stone lintel of the small southern doorway. Being at the back of the church as one normally approaches, it is hard to find, and in any case owes its fame solely to the story it was indented in the stone when Owain Glyndŵr threw his dagger at the church from the overhanging hill in a fit of anger.

The proximity of the church to the hotel defines the pair of them as the heart of old Corwen. A small bit of Welsh cultural history has its origins here, since it was in this substantial inn that the first National Eisteddfod took place, in 1789. A plaque by the door commemorates this seminal event (11a).

On the whole the area's associations lie much deeper in the past than that, and the shadow cast over it is undoubtedly that of the hero who gave his name to the hotel. This is the heart of the territory of Glyndŵr. Even his name associates him directly with the land he lived in, being taken, like the nearby town of Glyndyfrdwy, from the valley itself: 'the valley of the water of the Dee'. By birth Owain ap Gruffudd Fychan, born about 1359, the name by which he is known is, in the Welsh tradition, that of his territory.

Glyndŵr had estates in the area inherited from his aristocratic family, and

(12) Corwen's parish church, although located close to the town centre, has its own secluded setting.

(13) 'Owain Glyndŵr's Mount', probably a medieval motte, stands near the main road near Carrog.

III OWAIN GLYNDŴR

himself lived in palatial style at Carrog, midway between Corwen and Glyndyfrdwy, and at Sycharth, further south in the Tanat valley. His court bard, Iolo Goch, described for us his luxurious life there.

Nothing of these palaces, which were wooden structures, now survives, and the fine medieval motte which bears his name, 'Owain Glyndŵr's Mount', has no definite connection with him (13). It stands alongside the main A5 road not far from Carrog, and a short way away another ancient mound, known as Hen dom and marked on the map as 'Tumulus', is even more mysterious and unidentified. Glyndŵr's Mount, with its crown of trees and its profile against the sky, is suitably evocative, and if it is, as one may assume, the motte of a 12th century castle, then it was there in the chieftain's lifetime, known to, and maybe even used by him. The legend as told to George Borrow records that it was the site from which he would watch for his enemies coming from the Chester direction, and indeed if he did not do so he would have been foolish. The mount commands a perfect view of the river, the valley and the road.

Glyndŵr's two seats, at Carrog in Glyndyfrdwy and Sycharth further south, reflect his inheritance of two prosperous estates. Descended from the princes both of Powys and of Deheubarth in South Wales, he was a man of no slight substance. He studied law in London at the Inns of Court, and became a squire to the Earl of Arundel, the local Marcher Lord who at that time possessed Llangollen's castle of Dinas Brân. His early military training came with this apprenticeship to Arundel at his seat of Chirk Castle (14).

These are Marcher matters, and Owain was very much a part of the long-drawn-out state of tension on the border. His own background combines the two sides of the issue, since he was by geneology a part of independent Wales and by situation a Marcher Lord in the Norman mould himself. The immediate area in which he lived had experienced border tension since the time of King Offa of Mercia, whose famous dyke runs close to Chirk Castle. Henry I brought a formidable force through these valleys in 1114, and his grandson Henry II confronted the Welsh here again in 1165, at the battle of Crogen, again near Chirk Castle.

Between these wars and the time of Glyndŵr there occurred, of course, the invasion of Edward I which imposed on North Wales the Norman system of law and administration, and the feudal system, of which the concept of the Marcher lordships was an outcome. Power was devolved from the central monarchy to loyal and powerful lords, the stronger of which were given the areas of greatest dispute, such as this border country. In exchange for protecting these borders for the king by their occupation of them, they were able to build up their own influence and wealth.

Glyndŵr, as a man in such a position himself, had always been loyal to the English crown. He fought for Richard II in the Scottish campaigns, and his loyalty must have been tested when that monarch was deposed, once again

(14) The coat of arms of Owain Glyndŵr, reflecting his descent from the princely lines of Wales.

in North Wales, by the usurping Henry Bolingbroke, who then became Henry IV. Since Richard was taken as a prisoner from Flint to Chester, in 1399, he must have passed through Glyndŵr's own territory, and it is possible indeed that the chieftain was present at these critical events.

As well as Lord Arundel at Dinas Brân and Chirk, Owain had another powerful neighbour in the person of Lord Grey of Ruthin, who happened to be a friend of the new king's. Grey was autocratic, and, taking inadequate account of Glyndŵr's hot blood, he annexed to his territory a piece of moor which was probably traditionally common land, to which Glyndŵr also claimed a right.

This seemingly insignificant disagreement provided the detonator which fired the reserves of Welsh anger, and gave rise to one of the most tumultuous periods of Welsh history. When Owain's petition to Parliament was contemptuously rejected, and in the process he effectively became an outlaw, he decided to take the matter into his own hands.

Thus on 16th September in the year 1400 a company of his relatives and supporters met at his house on the Dee at Carrog, near Glyndyfrdwy, and proclaimed him Prince of Wales. They raised the flag of the Red Dragon, the banner of Cadwaladr, a traditional symbol of Welsh resistance. Glyndŵr was already forty-one years old, and nothing in his career so far could have foretold his heroic rebellion and his vision of a free Wales playing its role in a community of European nations. His name is still poetically connected with

III OWAIN GLYNDŴR

this dream and he has been called "the father of modern Welsh nationalism".

The nation rose as a whole to support him, and at once his troops invaded and destroyed Lord Grey's town of Ruthin. The fire of revolt swept outwards from there in all directions, and as it became clear that this was not just a minor local quarrel the King and the national army arrived in North Wales.

In no time at all another phenomenon had come into being: the legendary, rather than the real, Owain Glyndŵr. The familiar guerrilla tactics of the Welsh gave them greater mobility in the hill country, and Owain's ability to be apparently in several places at the same time soon gave him a reputation for magic in the eyes of the English.

The course and outcome of the war concern other parts of Wales and indeed Britain than the one we are at present in. Hopes soared for a time for the achievement of the free Wales which Owain aimed for, with its own Church and university, as he gained the powerful support of the Mortimers and the Earl of Northumberland, and finally of the King of France. English castles fell to his troops and manor houses were burnt throughout Wales.

The rebellion faded, however, as fast as it had flared up; the Welsh simply lacked the manpower and provisions to sustain it. As it became clear that he was hopelessly outnumbered his supporters compounded this situation by deserting him in hordes. The whole war lasted nine years, and in 1409 his headquarters of Harlech castle fell. His family was captured and he himself, now alone, disappeared into a Wales exhausted and destroyed by fire and famine. True to his legendary nature, he does not appear to have died. He turned up unexpectedly in various places during the next few years, until in 1413 no more is heard of him. He still appears to have been alive, however, in 1415, since Henry V, succeeding his father, offered him a free pardon. It is in character too that by way of Owain's son, Meredydd, the old hero refused it.

Owain's dream of a Wales restored to its former pride was premature. It was not until 1485 that Henry VII, descended from the house of Tudor which was related to Glyndŵr's own, raised again the standard of the Red Dragon on his march to the field of the Battle of Bosworth. Eventually the Tudor Act of Union of 1536 repealed the penal laws which all Welshmen suffered from after the Glyndŵr rebellion, but the whole of Wales remained absorbed as "part of England".

A popular and rather charming story mirrors these historical truths with the benefit of hindsight. One morning in the dawn mists the Abbot of Valle Crucis at Llangollen was walking in the Berwyn hills, and met Glyndŵr. The latter greeted him with the words 'You have risen early, Father'. 'No,' the Abbot sadly said, 'It is you who have risen early, by a hundred years.'

(15) The ruins of Dinas Brân on its round hill dominate the skyline in the country around Llangollen.

IV LLANGOLLEN

IGH on a round hill above Llangollen stand the jagged ruins of Dinas Brân, so elevated and isolated as to be continually silhouetted against the sky. It is a romantic feature, the stark imprint of human history in the natural lushness of the Dee valley, and its history and associations do justice to its visual effect (15).

Although connected (as is much in the area) with Eliseg, an early Prince of Powys, Dinas Brân enters history in its present form as the seat of a later prince, Madog ap Gruffudd, who reigned over Powys at the turn of the 12th to 13th centuries. His son, Gruffudd ap Madog, issued the charter of Valle Crucis from there in 1270. From the time of the Norman lordships, when other castles were coming into existence, it began to become neglected. Its owner then was John de Warrenne, Earl of Surrey, who controlled the border between his main seat at Oswestry and his new castle of Holt. It was because he found the latter more convenient than Dinas Brân that this old Welsh citadel began to fall into disrepair.

The castle's classically defendable position is obvious enough. A steep climb is required to reach it from almost all directions. A large-scale system of ditches and ramparts further protect its high walls, and one can still see the remains of a gatehouse and possibly a barbican to the east and the sturdy base of a tower half-way down the wall to the south. The narrow passage-way which was the original entrance is still intact (16). Dinas Brân, even in the shape of its present fragmented ruins, proclaims power and grandeur. It was, it is clear, a very substantial place. The two tall windows of the Great Hall on the south side look out over the Dee valley with a distinct air of dominance.

That these are no ordinary ruins is moreover proclaimed in legend. There are two quite separate indications that tradition has, at various times, identified this as no less than the Castle of the Holy Grail.

One element in the medieval stories about the Holy Grail was its connection with a 'Castle of Wonders', where travelling knights found themselves involved in strange adventures. 'Chastiel Brân' occurs as such a place in the story of the Norman outlaw Fulk Fitz Warine, himself a sort of prototype of Robin Hood. The second element connecting this castle with that of the Grail cycle of stories is its name.

'Brân' is simply the Welsh for 'crow', but it occurs also in Welsh mythology as the name of a deity, originally possibly a river god. Brân was the owner of a magic cauldron which could bring the dead back to life, which, like Ceridwen's cauldron of inspiration, is one of the roots of the mythical sacred vessel which became the Grail. He occurs again in later Grail stories as the 'Fisher King', whose name is several times given as 'Bron'.

(16) The entrance to Dinas Brân is through a narrow passage.

IV LLANGOLLEN

The stories of the Holy Grail come to us from these medieval origins in the form collected by Sir Thomas Malory, from both British and continental sources. When the castle where the sacred vessel is housed is first mentioned by Malory it is named as 'Corbin':

And so he departed, and rode till he came to the castle of Corbin.

Malory was translating from the French prose 'Lancelot' at this point, and it is surely no coincidence that 'Corbin' is an old French word for 'crow' or 'raven'. The castle of Corbin, the earliest form of the castle of the Holy Grail, was simply 'Dinas Brân' in French.

The story of Brân tells how his followers cut off his head when he finally fell in battle and took it to 'The White Mount' in London, where it formed a protection against invasion as long as it remained there. Interestingly the same is traditionally said of the ravens of the White Tower, indicating that perhaps they are the survival of a shrine of Brân there, his representatives no doubt because of their connection with his name.

It was Pennant who suggested that Dinas Brân was originally the seat of Eliseg, Prince of Powys, a name also surviving as that of the surrounding limestone escarpment, the Eliseg Rocks, and the quite unexpected Elizabethan half-timbered house near World's End, Plas Eliseg. The latter was for a time the home of Oliver Cromwell's brother-in-law, Colonel John Jones, who was one of the signatories of the death warrant of Charles I. It stands on the site of an earlier, and rather more legendary, court, that of Cadwgan, a Prince of Powys in the early 12th century. A popular story tells of the kidnap by his son Owain of the famous beauty Nest, daughter of the king of South Wales. His bringing her to this retreat led to a war which (because of Nest's former successes at the English court and her marriage to Gerald of Windsor, Earl of Pembroke) involved the Normans and King Henry I.

Both the house and the rocks above the valley are, confusingly, also sometimes known as Eglwyseg, meaning ecclesiastical, from their connection with the nearby Abbey; but modern spelling now tends to associate them rather with Eliseg the prince.

Most intriguing of all, in this connection, is undoubtedly the tall stone known as Eliseg's Pillar. It stands a little way up the hill from the ruins of the abbey of Valle Crucis, easily identifiable and near the road (17). Since the abbey and its valley take their name from it, 'the valley of the cross', it must at one time have had a cruciform head. It was apparently thrown down as being idolatrous during the Civil War, though we do not know whether it was intact before that.

The Eliseg Pillar is of interest as having been, when legible, the earliest post-Roman inscribed stone identified (17a). Pennant, in the 1770's, could

(17) Eliseg's Pillar stands prominently near the road which leaves Llangollen for the Horseshoe Pass.

(17a) An early example of an inscribed stone, the writing on its side has long ago ceased to be legible.

IV LLANGOLLEN

no longer read its inscription, but possessed a transcript made by Edward Llwyd. It tells us that it was set up by Eliseg's great-grandson in the ninth century:

> *Concenn filius Catelli, Catelli filius Brochmail, Brochmail filius Eliseg. . .*

and it then proceeds to trace Eliseg's own ancestry, through the British high-king Vortigern, who presided over the Saxon invasion, back to Roman times in the form of the usurping emperor Magnus Maximus. Pennant points out that the Brochmail mentioned as the grandfather of the pillar's erector was the Prince of Powys defeated at the battle of Chester in (he says) 607 A.D.

The pedigree of Eliseg thus recorded by his great-grandson should perhaps not be taken too literally. It was common for great rulers to invent for themselves an ancestry legitimising their position, and indeed many kings of that time traced their lineage back to gods. The tradition which it records, from this very early date, that Vortigern married a daughter of Maximus' occurs also in Geoffrey of Monmouth's 'History', and so reflects at least an accepted form of early British history.

The stone was at one time, Pennant again tells us, twelve feet high, now reduced to six; and a drawing he includes of it shows it in much its present form. He sees it as the direct successor of the pre-Christian standing stones, differing from them only in its shaped form and its inscription, they too being, in his view, memorials of the dead.

The Abbey which takes its name from the cross (in spite of being more correctly called Llanegwest) was founded in 1200 or 1201 by Madog ap Gruffudd, the current Prince of Powys. (18) It was a Cistercian house, an order which sought out peaceful and remote spots where they could be self-sufficient as a community. It grew to be a centre of Welsh religious life and was the burial place of its founder and his son Gruffudd and, it is said, of the poet Iolo Goch, who became the court bard of these princes' descendant, Owain Glyndŵr. George Borrow made a special pilgrimage to the Abbey ruins to see the famous poet's grave, but found when he got there that nobody there had even heard of him.

After a fire late in the century in which it was built, the Abbey was largely reconstructed, so that its ruins now date from the last part of the 13th century. The remaining fragment of its cruciform church still has a noble elegance, and extensive foundations of what was clearly a major complex remain to impress us with Llanegwest's former status. (16) It was of course brought to its present destroyed state following the Dissolution of the Monasteries in the time of Henry VIII. Now the Abbot's house, restored, houses a display, and a pleasant picnic area is established by the fishpond,

(18) Valle Crucis Abbey lies in an idyllic setting above Llangollen.

(19) The ruins of Valle Crucis Abbey still retain an air of grandeur and elegance.

IV LLANGOLLEN

which, incidentally, is the only surviving monastic fishpond in Wales. (19)

With this depth of history surrounding it, it is hardly surprising that Llangollen itself is an old and well-established town. Essentially a convenient crossing-point of the Dee, it clearly grew up around its bridge. That is said to date originally from the 14th century and so held to be the oldest stone-built bridge in Wales. In its present form largely a 15th century structure, set up by a Bishop of St Asaph, it is an impressive feature in itself. (20) Many of the inns and houses date from the 17th and 18th century, demonstrating that Llangollen was rich and important before the construction of the road which now runs through it. In fact it was a centre of the wool industry, like Bala, and there were times in British history when that association was enough to guarantee success.

The name derives from that of the patron saint of its church, St Collen, about whom more is known in legend than in fact. Collen's hagiography states that he was a British mercenary in the Roman army. Returning to Britain he became Abbot of Glastonbury, and it is of him that the strange tale is told of the appearance of the castle of Gwyn ap Nudd, king of the otherworld, on top of Glastonbury Tor. St Collen, who has denied the existence of the fairies, is summoned by their king to meet him at his castle there. When sprinkled with the holy water which Collen wisely brought with him the king, his castle and the attendant spirits disappeared. This story has a strange ambivalence, no doubt intending to represent the triumph of early Christianity over paganism but still conveying a latent belief in the world of spirits, since you cannot sprinkle with holy water something which was never there. Unfortunately it does not go on to explain how Collen then came to found a church so far away from these events, in the peace of the Dee valley.

The church (21) is of interest and importance for its remarkable carved ceiling, a most elaborate piece of work thought to date from the early 16th century. Richly carved in deep-coloured oak it displays a great wealth of detail in the form of figures of angels and gargoyle-like bosses, as well as the complex ornate pannelling of the vault itself (21a). The tradition that it came from Valle Crucis is now discounted since it is of the wrong size and form, but the commissioning of such skilled craftsmanship poses a mystery, and if a part of the explanation is that it owes its existence to the great wealth of the Abbey, then it must date from before 1535, the date of the Dissolution.

St Collen founded his 'llan' here in the sixth century, although of course nothing remains of the original building, which would have been a wattle structure. The present church is old, and contains many other interesting features, such as the mid-14th century doorway to the choir vestry.

Llangollen had, we can see, survived a long period of varied history before it entered its present role, as touring and cultural centre for this important area of North Wales. As the old coaching inns testify, that character had started to develop even before Telford built his road in the

(20) The bridge at Llangollen now dating largely from the 15th century, is said to be the oldest stone-built bridge in Wales.

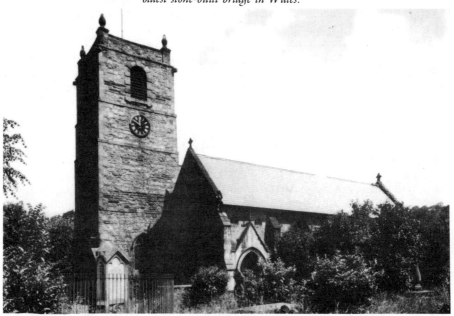

(21) The Parish Church of St Collen gives Llangollen its name.
Parts of it date from the 16th century.

IV LLANGOLLEN

1820's. We must remember that the A5 was not as innovatory here as in some other stretches of its route, and Llangollen was on a main coaching route before its construction. Thus distinguished travellers would inevitably stop here on their way to Ireland, and a bonus for doing so seems to have been the opportunity to visit the 'Ladies of Llangollen', themselves a strange phenomenon which can only be explained by the romantic tendencies of the time. No-one can ever have set out with less success to become recluses; they seem to have had a constant stream of visitors.

Lady Eleanor Butler was from a distinguished Irish Catholic family, related to the Duke of Ormonde. Sarah Ponsonby was also of genteel stock, though personally impoverished; her grandfather was a general. The two girls met when Sarah went to school in Kilkenny, when she was thirteen and Lady Eleanor twenty-nine. A romantic friendship developed out of their mutual dissatisfaction with their lives at home. In 1778 they ran away.

The first time they were apprehended by their families, but later that year they succeeded in getting consent to leave Ireland for Wales, and in due course settled in lodgings in Llangollen. They liked the town so much that they decided to rent a cottage, Pen-y-Maes, which they set about improving and renamed Plas Newydd (22).

On the face of it there is nothing particularly interesting about either the lives or the characters of these two eccentrics, and it is difficult to see why their fame was so widespread or their visitors so distinguished. They lived intentionally quiet lives, away from social interference, almost never leaving Plas Newydd for more than a day. Their main occupations were writing letters, reading, and tending the improvements of their house and garden. They corresponded with Edmund Burke, Lord Byron, Lord Castlereagh and George Canning. They dressed in identical outfits of black riding clothes with top hats, and assuming the portraits of them to be as flattering as possible they were certainly no beauties. In spite of these several discouragements they were visited by the great and famous, including the Duke of Gloucester, William Wordsworth, Sir Walter Scott, and no less a person than the Duke of Wellington.

The house and its setting provide some element of explanation. In the distance is a view of Dinas Brân, and wooded hillsides hide any sight of the town in between. The gardens and grounds fall to a dell bearing a tributary of the Dee, the Cyflymen. The seclusion and the subtle way the organised landscape merges with natural country give an immediate sense of peacefulness. Wordsworth, who had a feeling for nature perhaps greater than for verse, wrote a poem in the grounds:

A stream to mingle with your favourite Dee,
Along the Vale of Meditation flows. . .

(21a) The wooden panelling of the vaulted roof is a major feature of St Collen's Church.

(22) Plas Newydd, home of the 'Ladies of Llangollen'.

IV LLANGOLLEN

The ladies, being highly literate, were evidently discerning critics, since they are reported as saying that they could write better poetry themselves. They also took exception to a patronising reference later in the doggerel to their house:

> . . .*where faituful to a low roofed Cot*
> *On Deva's banks, ye have abode so long.* . .

Wordsworth was not invited again. Yet the cottage was at the time quite small, though not particularly aptly termed 'low roofed', and one wonders how it accommodated the rich and royal with, presumably, their servants. It was extended by the addition of wings by later owners, and these were removed as unsound in 1963 to restore the house to much the finished form in which the ladies left it. When Lady Eleanor died in 1829 they had been there together for nearly fifty years, and Sarah Ponsonby remained there alone for a further two before dying herself.

The main attraction of the house is its wealth of oak carvings (23), the customany gifts of their eminent visitors, and its grounds, which fall steeply to the gurgling stream. The whole has a pleasing atmosphere of intimacy. The property changed hands a number of times after the demise of the Ladies, until bought by the District Council in 1932.

The new road did not immediately alter the idyllic character which attracted the Romantics to Llangollen. George Borrow stayed in the town for some time in 1854 and recorded it in some detail as it was then: "a small town or large village of white houses with slate roofs." Borrow (24) was a native of Norfolk who had trained himself as a linguist and was by temperament nomadic, being particularly fond of the company of gypsies. His early wanderings gave us his books *Lavengro* and *Romany Rye. The Bible in Spain*, published in 1842, brought him widespread fame. He was a great walker, and *Wild Wales* was the result of a series of walks he made through Wales, from a base at Llangollen where he left his wife and daughter in a rented cottage, in the summer of 1854.

By the end of that century, A.G. Bradley remarked, in his invaluable *Highways and By-ways in North Wales*, that there was a visible rise in population in the August holidays: "traps and even the fearsome char-a-banc invade the leafy lanes". In the meantime much had happened; Llangollen had undergone the change brought about by radical improvement of road travel which North Wales as a whole has found, from time to time and now once again, is the equivalent of a social revolution.

(23) The wealth of oak carvings which decorate the interior of Plas Newydd is thanks to the custom of their many rich visitors bringing them as gifts.

(24) George Borrow, an adventurous traveller whose writing give us a fascinating insight into mid-19th century Wales.

V THOMAS TELFORD

LANGOLLEN, as we have seen, is an old coaching town of medieval origin owing something of its prominence to the chance of lying on a convenient route from England into Wales. The defile of the Dee valley forms a sheltered pass between, roughly speaking, the Berwyns and their foothills to the south and the Clwydian range with its moorland flanks to the north.

An established coaching route from Llangollen to Llanrwst in the Conwy valley, and thence on, via Conwy, to Anglesey and Ireland, was in use from the late 18th century. Shrewsbury formed the main posting point on the English side, and originally coaches ran from there via Wrexham and Mold to St Asaph, thence to Conwy. The deviation to Llangollen is first noted in 1776, and with the exception of an upland stretch between Pentrefoelas and Llanrwst, via Nebo, it followed much the valley route we take today. It was when a road was finally carved through the Snowdonia mountains by Lord Penrhyn in 1791, in the form of the Nant Ffrancon pass, and shortly afterwards extended to Capel Curig, that an alternative route became apparent.

In 1802 an Act of Parliament established the first turnpike to extend all the way from the coast at Llandegai to Pentrefoelas, by way of Capel Curig and Betws-y-coed. Here we have the origin of the A5; the all-important mail coach ran along it from the year 1808. It was shortly after this that the first Parliamentary Committee sat to consider the question of the harbour at Holyhead and the approaches to it.

Thomas Telford had been working on roads in the Scottish Highlands during the first years of the 19th century, and had established a considerable reputation as a civil engineer. The section of the Irish road between Shrewsbury and Holyhead remained inferior to the Midlands sections, maintained by their more affluent turnpike trusts. It became of national importance with the Act of Union between Britain and Ireland in 1800, since this involved the frequent travel of Irish Members of Parliament between Dublin and London. One such was Sir Henry Parnell, an admirer of Telford's, who was to play a decisive role in promoting the scheme, but originally pressure from the Irish Chancellor of the Exchequer, John Foster, brought the matter before a House of Commons Committee, in 1810. The Committee appointed Telford to make a survey of this stretch of road.

In April 1811 he reported. He recommended improving the route:

"from the English plains, where the river Dee leaves the mountains, at the bottom of the valley of Llangollen, and from thence to ascend along the south side of that river to the town of Corwen. . ."

35

(25) Thomas Telford, whose great engineering works are a spectacular feature in the Llangollen area.

V THOMAS TELFORD

rather than seeking a new route through the Berwyn range.

It was some years before these recommendations were translated into action, but in 1815 Parnell persuaded the government to allocate £20,000 to the Welsh section of the road. With Telford as engineer work proceeded first on the worst sections, from 1817 to 1820. In 1821 the toll-houses of the Llangollen section opened for business.

The initial effect was a sharp increase in Llangollen's facilities and population, its success as a coaching centre becoming apparent by the 1830s and early '40s. This brief flourishing was sharply curtailed by the rise of the rival road via Chester and the construction of a railway along the northern coast in the mid-1840s, which perhaps explains why Llangollen was still a modest place when Borrow was there in 1854.

Thomas Telford (25) was born in Dumfriesshire in Scotland in 1757, the son of a shepherd. His father died young and Thomas had a poor childhood. He left school aged fourteen and became a stonemason's apprentice. Via Edinburgh and London he progressed as a stonemason towards an interest in architecture, and the launching point of his career came with his move to Shrewsbury to undertake the improvements to Shrewsbury Castle, a piece of good fortune arranged by the Member of Parliament, Sir William Pulteney, who was a fellow-countryman of Telford's. He undertook many works in and around Shrewsbury, including the rebuilding of the jail to its present form, and in 1787, with his appointment as Surveyor of Public Works for the county, came the decisive move from architecture towards civil engineering.

Bridges and canals formed the foundations of his fame. We have to see his life in the context of a sudden revolution in the transport of goods and people. This in itself resulted from the technological advances which had brought about, and been further encouraged by, the Industrial Revolution. The invention of mass-production in industry gave rise to the commerce between production and its market, so familiar to us now in the days of the to-and-fro of container waggons, but which had previously been very much more localised. With this rise in commerce the mail became of national economic importance, while goods had to be conveyed in greater bulk.

Canals owed their early and striking success to the fact that the sole source of power for transport was still the horse. Because a weight suspended in water can be more easily moved than one resting on wheels, more goods could be moved further per horsepower on the new canals than on the new turnpike roads.

Both forms, for efficiency, had to be as level as possible, and hence the problem for the engineers at the beginning of the 19th century was to create a horizontal line through undulating country. Bridges, viaducts and aqueducts are the typical products of this time.

Telford's particular genius seems to have lain in his ability to combine a

(26) Pontcysyllte, near Llangollen, considered to be one of Telford's greatest achievements.

(26a) Telford used an innovatory technique, transporting the canal in a cast-iron trough.

(27) The Ty-isaf toll-house near Llangollen shows the architectural skill and care which Telford used in his personal design for all his structures.

(27a) Telford's drawing of the design of a toll-house on the Holyhead road.

V THOMAS TELFORD

meticulous attention to detail with a breathtakingly courageous imagination. His early training as a stonemason and his real vocation as an architect showed through all his work. The great elegance of the viaducts and aqueducts together with the radical attack on the problem typifies Telford.

Pontcysyllte, which lies within our area, is an excellent example (26). Faced with the problem of conveying the Ellesmere canal across the Dee valley, Telford went straight across: 121 feet above the ground, it makes its leap of 1007 feet in a trough of cast-iron plates (26a) carried on a stone structure supported by eighteen slender pillars. It is undoubtedly one of his finest works, and has earned repeated praise, but it is all the more remarkable from an engineering point of view for its innovatory technique. A cast-iron trough had been used once before, on the Shrewsbury canal, but to prove the effectiveness of this method on such a grand scale set a precedent for future constructions.

Pontcysyllte was built over a period of ten years, for a cost of £47,018. Apart from the renewal of the railings, faithfully copied from the original, it remains as Telford built it in the first years of the last century. It was opened in 1805 with a ceremony attended by an estimated 8,000 people.

As massive a task as the construction of Pontcysyllte was the embankment which was necessary to convey the canal to the aqueduct. Stretching out 1500 feet from the south bank of the valley, it forms a clearly gigantic undertaking. With typical ingenuity Telford linked this work with another solution to obstruction, the cutting on the approach to Chirk, transferring the material from the one to the other by boat.

Less obviously spectacular than these canal works is the road itself, now the A5. Although he employed an assistant and four inspectors to build this stretch of the Holyhead road, Telford planned and supervised every detail of the project himself. His eye as an architect is apparent wherever a structure became necessary, since he designed the milestones, the toll-gates (none of which remain in this area) and of course the toll-houses themselves (27) and (27a).

Remarkably parts of the A5, in its day the equivalent of a motorway, remain the same width as Telford built it. On these stretches one can see his characteristic walls, identifiable by the regular provision of bays in which repair material might be stored (28).

We are indeed lucky that this remarkable man was not simply a civil engineer but a man of vision and refinement as well. Clearly he loved his work and seems to have possessed an enviable temperament. Robert Southey, the poet and writer, who accompanied him on a survey of the

(28) Bays set into the original wall indicate the stretches of the A5 which remain today as Telford built them.

V THOMAS TELFORD

Highlands and became his friend, writes in glowing terms:

> *There is much intelligence in his countenance, so much frankness,
> kindness and hilarity about him flowing from the never-failing
> well-spring of a happy nature, that I was upon cordial terms with him in
> five minutes. . . A man more heartily to be liked, more worthy to be
> esteemed and admired, I have never fallen in with. . .*

*The history of travel is represented at Llangollen
by its steam railway and canal museum.*

Postscript — Llangollen Today

It is largely as a result of the high quality of its involvement with travel that Llangollen town today possesses so many features of interest. The fact that it lies both on the river and on the canal has given it an aquatic character, being now the focus of both canal trips and canoeing. A canal museum and the steam railway combine with the only slightly less relevant motor museum to emphasis locomotion. More recently the European Centre for Folk Studies has firmly established it as a cultural focus as well; its exhibitions and courses are complemented by an excellent library. At the same time Llangollen remains very much the posting-point it always was, providing a stopping-off point for trips into Snowdonia, a convenient spot to break a journey between England and the heartland of North Wales. Most famously of all, of course, literally all over the world, it is the home of the International Eisteddfod, founded in a modest way in 1946 and now drawing travellers in their masses to enjoy a feast of folk-music in a perfect setting. Even outside this highlight of the summer, Telford's Holyhead road is busier now than he could have foreseen, with people of all nationalities drawn to Llangollen's undoubted charm.

Llangollen is best known throughout the world for the International Eisteddfod which takes place there every July.

ACKNOWLEDGEMENTS

for illustrations on the following pages:

THE AUTHOR
4 (top); 6 (bottom); 8; 10 (bottom); 16 (inset); 18 (bottom);
24 (bottom); 26 (top); 28; 30 (top); 34 (top); 38 (bottom); 39 (bottom); 40; 42.

E. EMRYS JONES
4 (bottom); 12; 16 (bottom); 18 (top); 30 (bottom); 44 (bottom).

CAMBRIDGE UNIVERSITY
6 (top); 10 (top); 22.

BALA LAKE RAILWAY
14 (bottom) - Photo by Pete Briddon

NATIONAL MONUMENTS RECORD FOR WALES
16 (top; 24 (top); 32; 38 (top); 39 (top).

CLWYD ARCHIVES
26 (bottom)

NATIONAL PORTRAIT GALLERY
34 (bottom); 36.

LLANGOLLEN RAILWAY MUSEUM
44 (top) - Photo by Brian Dobbs.

LLANGOLLEN INTERNATIONAL EISTEDDFOD
45 - Photo by J.A. Pedder-Roberts

Map: Ken Gruffydd